One

Also by Serge Patrice Thibodeau

Poetry
La septième chute (1990)
Le cycle de Prague (1992)
Le passage des glaces (1992)
Nous, l'étranger (1995)
Le quatuor de l'errance suivi de la traversée (1995)
Dans la cité suivi de Pacifica (1997)
Nocturnes (1997)
Le roseau (2000)
Du haut de mon arbre (2002)
Seuils (2002)
Que repose (2004)
Seul on est (2006)

Prose
L'appel des mots. Lecture de Saint-Denys-Garneau (1993)
La disgrâce de l'humanité (1999)
Lieux cachés (2005)

In English
Let Rest (2005) *translation of* Que repose *by Jonathan Kaplansky*

One

Serge Patrice Thibodeau

a translation of *Seul on est*
by Jo-Anne Elder

Copyright © 2009 by Goose Lane Editions.
Original French version copyright © 2006 by Éditions Perce-Neige.
Originally published in French as *Seul on est*.

The epigraph on page 9 is from *Paul Valéry. Cahiers/Notebooks 2*, a translation of *Cahiers*, edited by Judith Robinson-Valéry, by Rachel Killick, Robert Pickering, Norma Rinsler, Stephen Romer and Brian Stimpson. Edited by Brian Stimpson. Peter Lang GmbH, 2000. Reprinted with permission.

Translated by Jo-Anne Elder.
Edited by Ross Leckie and Susanne Alexander.
Cover photo: "Flood at Bloomfield, New Brunswick" (detail), 2008, by James Wilson, www.jameswilson.ca.
Cover design by Julie Scriver.
Book design by Kent Fackenthall.
Printed in Canada
10 9 8 7 6 5 4 3 2 1

Library and Archives Canada Cataloguing in Publication

Thibodeau, Serge Patrice, 1959-
    One / Serge Patrice Thibodeau; translated by Jo-Anne Elder.

Poems.
Translation of: Seul on est.
ISBN 978-0-86492-533-6

    I. Elder, Jo-Anne. II. Title.

PS8589.H4436S48313 2009   C841'.54   C2008-908068-8

Goose Lane Editions acknowledges the financial support of the Canada Council for the Arts, the Government of Canada through the Book Publishing Industry Development Program (BPIDP), and the New Brunswick Department of Wellness, Culture, and Sport for its publishing activities.

Goose Lane Editions
Suite 330, 500 Beaverbrook Court | Fredericton, NB | CANADA E3B 5X4 | www.gooselane.com

To my sister Lise

Translator's Note

Serge Patrice Thibodeau wrote the poems in this collection in Moncton over a twenty-month period. A dedicated walker, he was often inspired by his explorations of the region around him and its connections and contrasts with other landscapes he had discovered, especially during his travels in Europe.

In *Seul on est*, the poet traces the path of the Petitcodiac River, observed through all the seasons as it makes its way into Shepody Bay at Hopewell Cape. In Moncton, waves travelling on the crests of the massive tides sent upstream to the Petitcodiac from the Bay of Fundy form a tidal bore, a natural phenomenon in which the leading edge of the incoming tide forms a wave of water that travels against the direction of the current.

In French, the tidal bore is called the mascaret. It is believed that this Gascon word comes from either "mascara" (for the dark coats of animals charging forward as the river does) or, as I would prefer to believe, from "mascarite." The same word gives us "magic" and "masquerade" in English.

In this translation, I have chosen to keep the French name for the mascaret, both because of the sound the word evokes (something not found in "tidal bore") and to honour the older names of Acadie by giving them a new place in English-Canadian poetry.

Jo-Anne Elder
Fredericton, 2009

Total embrace of the good and the better, struggle that swells,

Mixing; alone, one returns; alone, one rises

Alone one thinks no more, alone one has will, alone one is.

> Paul Valéry, "Poems and Short Abstract Poems,"
> *Cahiers/Notebooks 2*, translated by Stephen Romer

One

Stories given voice: the tides of the mascaret at dawn, its ice bronze;

alone, one hears all the voices, silent before the exquisite,

facing the blizzard, entering it, penetrating the breath

of the whirling white joy that slips between the pages

      of a book open wide

      into the gaping sphere,

      — luminescent as a desert isle —

      a one-bodied pulse

      at its centre.

No root can perish, time barely moves; threads of grass,

strands of salt or sun caught between its fingers, underground,

where everything moves, where the world begins again, wild and giddy,

where everything pauses and stirs to rhythms that cannot be altered,

> embers as far as the eye can see,
> to the island that holds the horizon
> — against the current of the Deportation —
> high on the cliff before the church caught
> between the everlasting and the evergreen of Pointe-Sapin.

Everything connects, nothing keeps the dispersed bodies from reuniting,

earth is left a legacy of love for the exquisite, even if one is reborn alone;

at night, especially, knowing that sight stretches out, alone, from within,

going back over one's steps, musky leaf-mould along the shore,

> making a bed in its own nest,
> underbrush, undersea, undergrowth,
> — at night, one can see nothing but the whole —
> for as long as it takes to gather
> goodness.

Naked, on the ground, incantatory white, a flock of mallards shifts, merges
for a moment with a remnant of blue; the sounds of the marsh under the snow
vibrating, articulate chime in the ear, absorbing its attention,
until only the compelling refrain lingers:

> no, not again, no longer;
> what has been torn away,
> — bark from the water, sap from the rock —
> all this breathes once more,
> and no one has to depart again.

What was torn from the flesh, all of it returns, settles, lodges

in the veins, the troubled tides, for alone one is sound, alone

one is word, alone one awaits the inevitable return of the churning tides;

balanced on the back of a mother burdened and worn, one

is dying to love, dying to begin again,

everything repeating and rebounding

— tirelessly —

in the circle of mystery,

mad with the most precious complicity.

A pine, head first in the ground, brandishes its roots, offers them

to the stars, its branches digging into the entrails

of cities, countering the circulation of insects, the radiation

of metals; a bottle crashes on the marble tiles

      of the ocean floor,

      a message empties itself out

      — a humble metaphor for forgetting —

      and unfurls its ribbed foliage,

      its illegible constellations.

Light, a simple sketch of the whole, an awkward spectre;

those fool enough to try to grasp it might as well adjust, for it takes root

wherever it wishes: on the open sea, especially, after the passage of ships,

when the dolphins leap in the bay and the whales

       capsize; in prisons

       they have sawn through the bars;

       — a smouldering wildfire of weeds —

       they have closed the shutters

       and imitated daylight.

But red is the cloak of fire, red is the cloak crossing

our path, no red light stops it, neither the devil nor the deep blue sea.

Who stole the horses? Who savaged the land? Who burned down the barns?

No matter, those brash enough to raise their heads received the brand

        of history; now, the silhouette

        of a god so fictive and naive

        — set to the chants of formless winds —

        emerges, brazen-faced, from the fog,

        frightened by its own reflection.

One forgets; one *wishes* to forget: the past, those who have passed on,

a breath; the mascaret draws in memories with the tide only for those

who venture into the water unwitnessed, lost time welling up in the throat,

and the eye, seeing nothing, is sown, sprouts, blossoms;

        an abandoned lighthouse,

        the aftertaste of having loved,

        — loved whom? whose one and only? —

        the salt meadow quenches thirst,

        the echo persisting through fields of wheat.

Twenty degrees below zero, under the ice the stream crosses the marsh
and refuses to freeze, winding through the city, intrepid, a Mozart sonata;
under fingertips, the burning body melts, under the covers, unashamed;
firm, seductive, smooth, a discreet light uncovers no one;

>the breaking waves of syllables
>call to mind
>— the fuse of a simple genesis? —
>a life so infinitely small,
>unaware of its existence.

Here, the ice brings a memory to the tip of its tongue, chestnuts roasting

on charcoal in Barcelona, on Las Ramblas, in front of a bookstore,

a few euros in a pocket, a hunched-over woman given a yogurt,

a baguette, a piece of cheese and a coffee; thank you, she says

        to the stranger,

        and she walks off

        — anything but indifferent —

        without a worry

        about her next meal.

Her image disappears from the eyes of a couple in love; the picture
stutters, giving only hints, an illusion: no face, no profile, nor any
particular build, just muscular, rolling shoulders, no shape, no hips,
without a song; outside, a scrap of paper has become stuck

      between two bars, the nightjar
      slips in, takes off;
      — night and day, the wind comes to the wrong door —
      no one knows what tugs on the roots
      and fills them with the desire to leave.

The night also accepts that the ocean can rise up in a single leap

and, in its anger, change course, retrace its steps,

and that the sky, exhausted, can fall flat on top of the undergrowth,

the shoreline dishevelled, the branches of the first tree that happens by

        splayed, the wind refusing

        to backtrack;

        — the advent of chaos? in whose judgment? —

        elsewhere, a fish-eyed predator lying in wait

        predicts the coming of the enemy.

The snow falls without ceasing; behind all the white, the sun
dazzles once again as if for the first time, as if time is moving backwards,
so that one's gaze surrenders to its exquisite majesty; time catches the light,
the shape of the house across the street has shifted, windows keep watch;

the tree, motionless,

a mountain-ash,

— a white sound hides within —

and encircled above,

Cygnus, the constellation of the swan.

The ice flows upstream, against the current,

so it was written; our astonishment transforms gravity;

the same image at the source of the wind's sweep

has reached the lips, has been placed at the fingertips;

       at the edge

       all is calm,

       — taken refuge, stones dispersed —

       the truly white and the truly exquisite

       unite.

Light carved between slate cliffs and wild ice floes,

the hidden face of a naked body under its tongue, the palm of a hand

restless, stretching out, craves a tangible offering,

so that a simple refrain, a shiver, can creep into the small of its back;

discomfort and distress

brushed away,

— flesh curves in wonder —

an unending song rises up,

gently draws the lips together.

·

One is alone when the sun sets and the white no longer glows,

and alone one moves forward when time has come to draw from the well,

on an airport runway lost amid the spruce trees and marshes, salt everywhere,

and within the body whirls desire and hunger, another season coming to an end;

> the impertinent scent
>
> of spring
>
> — an earthy voice between sky and sea —
>
> slips in between the sheets,
>
> licks its hands clean.

The question of the exquisite, one *would wish* to solve painlessly,

the mystery on its lips, alone, one *would love* to surrender oneself completely

to its song, to make contact anew: to stroke, hug, embrace its image,

carry it carefully in an inside pocket, away from pale windows and doors;

> and those eyes!
> the wind is suspended,
> — everything leaning —
> breathing slows
> on the way up the hill.

Learning to *sustain* the gaze in the presence of the exquisite, love,

with the eyes, one's own and those of the other, it's possible; it's possible then

and will never be impossible again, an unbreakable thread of earth as rare

as it is tenacious; the eyelids, heavy, hiding the blue iris,

> the heroic cast
> of the jaw,
> — what did solitude mean? —
> and roots spread
> as broad as shoulders.

Naked in his hotel room, the traveller slowly sips his coffee;

the clock strikes the hour in the belfry of Saint-Nicolas-des-Champs;

Chopin in the courtyard; away from home in search of freedom, for alone

one is free, able to settle one's accounts with life, on the road;

       the exquisite, its motionless charm

       and insistent appeal, the exquisite

       — eyes etched with scenes from history —

       unfurled, unveiled, volatile, a vessel heeding

       no warning.

Two bald eagles have made their nest in a village;

at the same moment, by chance and unhurried,

someone is born, nameless and nearly voiceless, in a place where

the ferns grow tall after spring's green floods

    have drenched the light soil with promises

    that sink to the threshold of the untenable;

    — waiting for the sunflowers to bloom —

    a face turns slowly to the sky, offering itself to the stars,

    and sea-breezes smooth its skin.

Under the plane trees, under the palm trees, before the hibiscus,

in front of the crumbling facades of unending boulevards,

the generous lips of the exquisite humbly murmur

tales of wonder, its silhouette in the cushioned hollows of a bolster,

       having finally crossed the mirror

       from one side to the other; a wounded voice

       — the fleeting sky has taken root —

       carves out a place in the shadows,

       its foot planted squarely upon a cloud.

It is said: man is born to betray his own,

to sign the confession of his acts, to contemplate nothingness,

his unique creation, another way to stick out his tongue, kneeling,

black stripes knotted around his neck, a serpent in his fist,

       eyes thick with yellow,

       mouth ready to utter the last judgment,

       — soul stranded on the sandy floor of the arena —

       weapon aimed and ready when the time comes

       to fire on his neighbour.

The city is empty of song, the grounded plane risks being swept away

in the winds and, in November sadness, the spruce trees

gather the reflections that fall from the clouds, and the black heads

of the chickadees have drifted away, deserted the manger,

      the measures of their songs vanished into the air;

      the trail, arms crossed in the river's mud,

      — a dolphin rescued, at noon, downtown —

      the water catches its breath,

      arches around the bend.

An attitude, while listening,

sets the image back in place, and the sound

from where it comes and from which it arises;

it's the television scanning the street,

> the all-exposed, the never-naked,
>
> playing out, one pixel at a time,
>
> — the tree trunk has narrowed —
>
> the sloped, washed-out roof,
>
> the slanted spine of the horizon.

Atlantic filet of sole, Madagascan
fleur de sel and spicy Espelette pepper,
hands extended, Bartoli's voice,
streets intersected by sheets of rain,

Mendoza wines, secrets held close,
the long-remembered taste of the absinthe of Gascogne,
— in the evening, around the table, another story, candles burning —
Basque country; what is called a nation
stands upright along the footbridges.

And then it happens. Whatever has chased away
the American bittern has not been named;
the fire in the cattails and the beggar
have brought the world back home again,

>non-stop, a strange flight
>never taken by strangers,
>— and the beginning? the centre? —
>tired, beyond gravity, in the front-row seats,
>with a perfect view as we surge forward.

No one wonders about himself in front of the mirror

in a room dizzy with light, no one,

and it is not summer; only the knots

in the wood floor gleam;

        the nervous white of the winds,

        Sunday stuck between a die's one and six,

        — a round table of sandblasted glass —

        and covering their surfaces, the ice

        prevents the dice from rolling.

In the marsh, the great blue heron distances itself

from everything that stands in the way

of light, from everything without reflection,

among the rusted cattails of autumn;

no one prevents the forest equinox

from curving toward the exquisite and the clearing,

— as for the landscape, it is reincarnated —

so that words may find tranquility,

and so that fires along the way may be snuffed out.

From here on, the road narrows; forgotten is
the forest, the texture of lichen, fresh water.
Everything is cut short. A drop of water, an oak leaf,
each with its many voices, enchanted and unique,

        trails floundering in the shadows,
        an invitation to lose oneself,
        — the forest blurs the footprints —
        a constellation half extinguished
        by a cloud gone astray.

So that streams can filter through the shadow's holes,

roots have lifted up the gravestone,

have broken it apart; now open, it gapes,

its silence as round as the sky,

      a moss-covered rock, dismembered,

      and an empty pit, a hollow womb;

      — a lamp under the bell —

      the timid darkness, a single thread,

      winds its way among the stones.

A tousled labyrinth, stones disordered
by the wind's well-equipped command,
points to the sky, tilts toward the ground,
flowers fading and crumbling, shapeless

        chrysanthemums, petals of oblivion,
        desert isles on a face,
        — one finds oneself alone, a gaze —
        and a path, and a valley, shallows,
        a shadow unknown to the horizon.

An earthen pot, a pot filled with earth,

the space shuttle threatened

by lightning, the gaunt pack ice,

a green lung collapses,

      as if nothing is happening,

      acting as if there's nothing to say;

      — a blade gleams, cuts through the dark —

      a thin strip of hope slips

      into a dislodged vault.

Heavy stone crosses have toppled down
from monuments, names blurred;
grass obscures them, presses against them, runs along
their bony contours in every direction;

       and the soil, it moves aside,
       absorbs the rock,
       — fallen from the sky, sprouting in the earth —
       summer, light, borderland
       of high noon.

Ocean, hermetically sealed space and fire

lit by a careful hand,

on every side, among bodies in chains,

the swoosh of the wind and the sword,

       while at the Père-Lachaise Cemetery,

       one can hear the sound of a truck backing up

       — a shovel carried on a shoulder —

       and the voice of an Airbus

       amplified by a cloud.

Alone there is death. One morning,

the razor labouring through the green,

at the moment of the mascaret, red,

somewhere, has started to spread, a moment

        of silence in the underbrush,

        a digital photo

        — it is coming forward, from the open sea —

        on the monitor,

        moss carrying lichen on its shoulders.

Hawkweed blooming along the rails,

the train moves from east to west,

full of slumber, from the seaport

to the envied metropolis; what can be seen of it,

       the distracted faces; one can hear

       night falling and heads nodding off,

       — outside, it's turning warm —

       an empty apartment,

       without a cozy corner or a fire.

On television, at rush hour,

the smell of a chicken coop, thawing manure,

waste spreading before our eyes; a superb display,

ugliness, mediocrity laid before us;

      grease, scum, dirt

      under the fingernails,

      — novelties of the Middle Ages —

      memory, indignant

      in its metal frame.

Worry, one might say, if one

were alone. Sunflowers

seen from the train, a thousand years of history,

an abandoned post office,

        Les Landes, vacant flatlands,

        sundial and compass,

        — destiny mapped out —

        inexhaustible geography,

        a single being.

The scarecrows are tired;

they get cold at night; their ragged clothes,

fraying at the seams, mimic the wind,

awkwardly melancholy,

> running out of breath; summer
>
> vanishes into the blue fog,
>
> — an expired passport, doubt —
>
> lighter luggage,
>
> flight in the heart, surging forward.

The exquisite, hovering above,

has come back with the autumn,

wearing a cap and a checked shirt,

an urban smile, a crow's foot,

       eyes lacquered blue,

       at the corner of its mouth, a dream,

       — dawn does not grow old —

       and the anticipation has been dispersed,

       a warm breath; it's time to celebrate.

Joy is in the air, being bandied about;
it's beginning again, seasons, joy
and everything hidden between the lines
of its hand, winding choreographies

        of time's passage,
        stained glass windows dimmed,
        — the poles suddenly attracting —
        a makeshift bridge
        under artillery shells.

The full moon of October; the exquisite,

goodness: they are another meaning for purity;

a shoreline, if necessary, a home,

a house that lets everything breeze in and out;

       farther away, around, across,

       above us, it's there,

       — because one is alone —

       counting backwards, the return of the earth

       underfoot.

Points of Reference

The poems in this collection were written in Moncton, New Brunswick, between January 2005 and September 2006. Some were published previously in French in *Exit* (issues 38 and 41) and *Estuaire* (issue 124). Others were published in Italian translations in *L'immaginazione*.

The author wishes to express his gratitude to the Canada Council for the Arts for its generous support during the writing of this book and to the Départment d'Études françaises, Université de Moncton, for providing him with the position of Writer-in-Residence during the winter of 2005.

The translator would like to express her gratitude towards Serge Patrice Thibodeau for his generous support and insightful comments and her sincere thanks to Susanne Alexander, Ross Leckie, Akoulina Connell, Julie Scriver and Kent Fackenthall, who made our translation into a truly beautiful book.

The Author

Serge Patrice Thibodeau is the author of a dozen collections of poetry, including *Le quatuor de l'errance* and *Seul on Est*, both of which won the Governor General's Award for poetry. He has also written numerous essays and, in 2004, an oratorio with composer Pierre Michaud entitled *Odysséa*, which commemorated the 400th anniversary of the founding of Acadie.

In addition to his two Governor General's Awards, Thibodeau has received numerous other honours, including the Prix France-Acadie in 1991, the Prix Edgar-Lespérance in 1994 and the Grand Prix du Festival international de la poésie de Trois-Rivières. He has also received the prestigious Prix Émile-Nelligan, the only Acadian to ever receive this award.

Thibodeau is the editorial director of Éditions Perce Neige in Moncton, NB. His poems have been translated into fourteen languages.

The Translator

Jo-Anne Elder is a writer, literary translator and the editor of *ellipse*. She has translated more than a dozen novels and story collections, including three with Fred Cogswell. She won the inaugural David Adams Richards prize for her story collection, *Postcards from Ex-Lovers*. Her translations have twice been finalists for the Governor General's Award and the Atlantic Poetry Prize.